Fairytale Fever Dream

Karina Rasner

Presentation by *BookLeaf Publishing*

Web: www.bookleafpub.com

E-mail: info@bookleafpub.com

ISBN: 9789358317909

First edition 2023

ACKNOWLEDGEMENT

I would like to thank my mom for bringing art and poetry into my life. Without her none of this would be possible. I want to thank all my friends who endlessly inspire me to keep writing even without knowing they are. I want to thank everyone who has ever listened to a poem of mine and showed me support. And most of all I would like to thank the people who have inspired these words to be written. Even if we do not talk anymore and have gone on our separate paths, our memories will live on forever through these poems. That makes it all worth it.

PREFACE

Art transcends cultural boundaries and connects humans of all generations and backgrounds. There are no black and white situations in life. Everything you go through is a complex web of time, people, conversations, and emotions. When you think you know someone, think about it, do you really? Do you know their traumas, and the trivial things that tick them off? Do you know the beautiful thoughts that are never spoken but forever on their mind? Well, these are mine, and now they are yours too. I hope that even one of these poems speaks to you, or makes you feel something. You can put 10 people in a room and have them all read the same poem, but each one will read it through their own unique lens. What do these poems mean to you?

Fairytale Fever Dream

My lipgloss shines under the sun,
I wait and wait, but there's no one…
But I have my lemon tea
And the book of poems I read at sea.
I love my skirts long or short,
I paint my eyes and never get bored.
I search piles of vintage clothes,
I love my moods - the high and lows.
I weave beads into my hair…
"That girl," they say,"is just so rare!"
But I just like the little things
My fairy doll hung by the wings,
Picking outfits one by one…
The sun might set, but I'm not done.
I belt out songs out of my range…
"That girl," they say, "is just so strange!"
But I just like the little things,
They knit your life with little strings.
When you go to sleep or are awake,
It's the small affairs that are at steak.
Don't lose sight hoping for more,
Then you will lose what came before.
I walk up to the mountain peak…
"That girl," they say, "is just so unique!"
But I just like the little things:

The lights, the cars, the silver rings…
My lipgloss shines under the sun,
I no longer wait just for anyone.

Unknown Length

We might lose hope, but never strength
Solving problems of unknown length.
Time goes by and it will end,
Cuts and bruises it might mend.
But when you want things to go back,
Courage and hope you will lack.
For healing hearts you need not strength,
But hope at an unknown length.
Tie together all your thoughts
And everything you ever fought,
And if you think you live a lie,
Fix it if you dare try.
But when you heal the wounds you make,
Oh, unknown strength that will take!

When The World Goes Dark

When the world goes dark we're left with our
thoughts,
We're left with the feelings the day has brought.

When the world goes dark we are rarely okay,
Thinking things that we dare not say.

When the moon is out and the high beams are
on,
We realize that yet another day is gone…

Another day of pretending, another day of lies,
Another day of fake smiles when we want to cry.

When the world wakes up, the cycle restarts,
And we go on pretending, cause that is our art.

And we count down the minutes till we are
alone,
Cause when the stars come out it changes the
tone.

Soon the sun goes down and our thoughts start
to spark
Oh how it hurts when the world goes dark.

Losing You

I'm not scared of being single,
I'm scared of losing you.
I'd cry for twenty hours,
If that was all that was left to do.

And I'm not scared of my own feelings,
But I'm scared that we are done,
Because a week ago you were my world,
And now my world has no sun.

And I find comfort in the crying,
In the pain, in the unknown,
But I feel like you gave up trying
The last time you hung up the phone.

And nobody will ever get it…
They say:"How were you in love with him?
You could do so much better!
Don't let your heart be so dim."

But they don't get the feeling
That I get when I see your eyes…
I see a budding future,
But, I guess, you see goodbyes.

And I'm not scared of being broken,
But I'm scared I won't be fixed,
Because I only see a few things wrong,
But maybe you have a list.

And three hundred sixty-six days ago
We were only just friends,
But now we are back there once again
Like it was some sort of trend.

And this seemed like it had potential,
One that we didn't pursue…
But I'm not scared of being single -
I'm scared of losing you.

Final Wave

The constant fear of not knowing
When is it going to end
The moment you wish you realized
Was the final of its wave

The walls are closing in
And you don't know how to climb
Is there torture in knowing
It's time to say goodbye.

Forced Love

I hear heartbeats in the silence…
Forced love, it feels like violence.
There's no corner I can hide in,
Nowhere I can run…
If you hate that you love me,
Why are we not done?

I feel whispers while I'm sleeping…
Stay quiet, but I'm bleeding.
I want to feel alive again,
My soul is mine no more…
If you hate that you love me,
Are you just keeping score?..

Unspoken

What is it that you think you know,
My deepest darkest thoughts?

The creeping ridges in my mind
      Lit up by a thousand watts.

I've lived a million lives,
      And I've died a million deaths…

So how do you know the unspoken words
      That get lost beneath my breath?

Wounds

Torture me with your words
I know you will anyway

Bruise me with your touch
I know that you won't stay

Wound me with your glance
I know you have no price

Harm me with your love
I know you won't think twice

Less

Am I somehow less human?
Less deserving of your grace?
Stumble on the rocks
Bones aching
End up in an unforgiving place.

Oh, I'm no worse, no braver,
No weaker,
Not looking for a cause to flee.
I've dug my roots in solid ground,
But to you there's scratch to see.

Am I somehow less alive?
Less aware of what's to come?
Live life by the book -
Heart breaking,
End up with a mind that's numb.

Oh, I'm just youthful, just open
Just yearning.
I'm looking for a place to be.
My eyes, my limbs, my torn-up mind
Are all composing me.

Don't divide me into layers,
Scrape away the burnt-out ash,
Dim my spark
Ignite a fire,
End up with the hollow flesh.

Am I somehow less human
Just because I'm craving more?
Exist among the wilting flowers,
But to flourish I implore!

Wholeness

I should feel broken
Somehow I feel fixed
Thought I'd be in a
Million pieces
But I'm whole

North

I got that summertime sadness
But it's winter now
Maybe it's repressed madness
Stuck in me somehow

Every year the time goes on
And with it goes the warmth
I just wish my mind could grasp
The beauty of the North

But every flake of snow
Reminds me of the past
The perfume I used back then
And how it didn't last

And every time I look
At the ever changing lights
I wonder if one day
I will truly be alright…

Empty

15

I was strong
I used my strength
To help the weak
Now I am empty

Beg

One day you will find me
And I won't have to beg
One day you will answer
        Without playing tag
One day I won't wonder
        If there is something
wrong with me
Am I too little or too much
        Too assured
                for you to see
One day you will want me
And it won't be a drag
One day you will love me
And I won't have to beg

Simple

People have dreams
All I wish is simple
I want to lay down
Close my eyes
And think
"I'm so happy"
then fall asleep.

Lavender

You were once my lavender,
But then you turned to gray,
Cause the words that hurt the most
Are the ones we didn't say.

Used to cry I'm the one that saved you,
But you're the one I need,
Because you're on to the next person,
While I'm the one that bleeds.

It's not the things you did,
It's the things you didn't do,
You forget that I exist,
And I still give thought to you.

If you don't water flowers,
Leave them dried up in the room,
Abandon them for hours,
They lose their will to bloom.

You were once my lavender,
But then you turned to gray.
Maybe our on and off attachment
Was designed to be erased.

Maybe I saved you,
But I'm not the one you need,
Guess I saw flowers
Instead of ever growing weeds.

For a while you had fixed me,
But it's been different now,
Didn't lose my faith completely,
But it's slowly wilting to brown.

Im learning to drive down those roads
That were once both of ours,
The valleys where we planted our roots
Are now filled with just my flowers.

You were once my lavender,
But then you turned to gray.
And our memories were like petals
born to fade and fall away.

We grew out of our pain,
So we grew out of each other.
You don't need me when you thrive -
Then I'm a weed, I'm just a bother

I'm glad if you are happy,
I just don't think you understand -
You're growing towards your own sun
Whose heat we can't withstand.

You need me when your wilting,
So you needed me all the time,
Then less and less, and off and on,
Until now, I guess, you're fine.

And once you were my lavender,
But then you turned to gray…
Next time you run out of light,
I won't share my ray.

Metro Tickets

I found our old metro tickets.
Yes, those we used last year.
We planned to come back one more time,
But we will not, I fear.

I found them in those jeans you liked.
Yes, those, the faded gray
Dusty on the basement floor,
Discarded til yesterday.

And I don't miss you anymore,
But one thing will always hurt…
I can't seem to recall your voice,
Or how you used to flirt.

So I will use our tickets,
Won't let them go to waste,
Walk the city by myself,
And let our memories get replaced.

Autumn Crested Fate

I told myself no
But that was before
The moon turned crescent shaped
Before I fell down
A glimmering track
Of autumn crested fate.
And one day I chased the wind
And left a little bit too late
I saw your face and I knew then
That it couldn't be erased.
And flaws dwindled away
Like moths without the light
In the trees
The stones
The crushed up leaves
I could see your eyes.

Soul To Skin

Talking in circles you can't find a cliff
change is in the air like the dust

I do this for myself and for the others
don't assume what's not yours to change

We've all hurt and bruised each other
purple only when there's passion

for it's not love unless you bleed
like skin when you care too much